Embracing
BRINGS YOU BACK

Embracing
BRINGS YOU BACK

PAT CLIFFORD

© Pat Clifford, 2006.

All rights reserved. No part of this publication may be reproduced, stored in a retrieval system or transmitted, in any form or by any means, without the prior written consent of the publisher or a licence from The Canadian Copyright Licensing Agency (Access Copyright). For an Access Copyright licence, visit www.accesscopyright.ca or call toll free to 1-800-893-5777.

Edited by Lorri Neilsen Glenn.
Cover design by Duncan Campbell.
Book design by Karen Steadman.
Cover image, Cover images: "Butterfly Wing," by Adalberto Rios Szalay/Sexto Sol, and "Cracks and stresses in ice, full frame Fludir, Iceland," by Stephen Toner/ Getty Images.
Printed and bound in Canada at Gauvin Press.

Library and Archives Canada Cataloguing in Publication

Clifford, Pat, 1947-
    Embracing brings you back / Pat Clifford.

Poems.
ISBN 1-55050-339-1

    1. Cancer--Poetry. I. Title.

PS8605.L565E42 2005   C811'.6   C2005-907233-4

1 2 3 4 5 6 7 8 9 10

2517 Victoria Ave.
Regina, Saskatchewan
Canada S4P 0T2

Available in Canada and the US from:
Fitzhenry & Whiteside
195 Allstate Parkway
Markham, Ontario
Canada L3R 4T8

The publisher gratefully acknowledges the financial assistance of the Saskatchewan Arts Board, the Canada Council for the Arts, the Government of Canada through the Book Publishing Industry Development Program (BPIDP), the Government of Saskatchewan, through the Cultural Industries Development Fund, and the City of Regina Arts Commission, for its publishing program.

For my mother, Jean Haidenger, with love.

Table of Contents

Introduction	i
Kissed Once, Indifferently	1
False Face Society	2
Bilingual	3
March 2002	5
Prairie girls get sunburns	7
The Mind of Death	11
Licked Into Shape: Winter Kill	12
Naming	13
Holding Emptiness	14
On Liz, Dying	15
Butterfly Effect	16
To sit among the rocks before I die and hear the ocean breathe	18
I look for little miracles these days	19
False Face: Rise	20
Sitting With Catherine	23
Hagiography	24
Against Time	26
Covered head	27
Kin	29
False Face: Clinic	31

Bald	35
Ragged purple scar	37
Drowning	38
Look Good, Feel Better	39
Hands	40
Terra intima	41
Mustard Gas	42
Venous Refusals	43
Sitting in a coffee shop, cold	47
Vowels	48
False Face: Bedside	49
Sometimes you miss people for the damndest reasons	50
Kathy, barrel-assing down a back road	51
Cold Comfort	52
Winter Clarity	53
Licked Into Shape: January Big Bear Moon	54
Acknowledgments	57

Introduction

She is a friend of my mind. She gather me, man. The pieces I am, she gather them and give them back to me in all the right order. It's good, you know, when you got a woman who is a friend of your mind. – TONI MORRISON

IN MARCH 2002 I was diagnosed with advanced ovarian cancer. Those words marked one of those turning points all of us have experienced in our own lives, when everything else becomes *after*: after your first kiss, your first period, your first lovemaking. After surgery, after chemotherapy, after losing my hair twice and growing it back again, after watching friends die, after learning a new body geography.

This has been an amazing time. In an earlier version of the manuscript, I contemplated having a section on cancer clichés: those pearls of wisdom that make me nuts because they are such easy currency – and because they are true. One of those clichés is that nobody ever gets cancer by themselves. As soon as the words are out of the doctor's mouth, everyone who loves you also has cancer in their lives, too.

And so I wish to acknowledge all those people whose lives have been transformed by the change in mine. It is a wide circle that radiates from the core of family and dearest friends, both men and women, who have been steadfast and fierce in their love and protection, keeping vigil in the lounge across from my hospital bed all night before I had my surgery; sitting with me through twenty rounds of chemotherapy and all the tests, scans and clinic visits that accompany them; singing me to sleep; swallowing their own fears and shock in the alien worlds into which I have been propelled; and braving those same fears and shock so we could explore this new terrain together; travelling and laughing and reading and celebrating small victories and large.

I am in love with words, not only with their sounds and shapes, but also with the ancestors whose ghosts hover just above the line. One of those words is *comfort*. The ancients knew, *con fortitude*, that comfort comes from being strong together, in good company. I have taken comfort in the strength of that intimate circle whose names I hold closest to my heart.

I have also taken comfort in the skill and care of doctors and nurses who dedicated their lives, long before me, to helping. Ovarian cancer is an intractable disease with a high rate of recurrence and mortality in the years immediately following diagnosis. I am deeply touched that the team of physicians and nurses who care for me chose this difficult specialty anyway, and remain open, compassionate and full of good humour in the face of all their losses, too. In particular, I would like to acknowledge Dr. Prafull Ghatage, who directs the work of the medical team who care for – and about – me. And I acknowledge Dr. Cheng Xia, whose work with far older forms of healing has kept me strong.

Many of the poems in this collection are elegies, lamentations for women I have known in the past three and a half years. I met them all through the support group that meets every Thursday afternoon at the Tom Baker Cancer Center. There have been 52 women in this group since shortly before I joined. 25 have died. Sometimes people wonder, and sometimes I do, too, why I persist in going. But every time I wanted to walk away, I was drawn back by the witness of their lives and deaths. Each of them has made the eyeblink passage we will all someday make: the very last time you let out a breath and your chest remains still forever.

I have learned much from them, not the least, that whatever comes to us can be lived eyes wide open.

Kissed Once, Indifferently

Left nearly breathless
by death I sit
now in the lengthening evening
light, a moon sliver dancing

with Venus. My outstretched arm yearns
and my two fingers make them appear
and die, appear and die.
In this sweet game

of hide and seek my own hand
is larger now than
all the world, and I lick
life's honey from a razor's edge

False Face Society

The Iroquois of the eastern Great Lakes made
masks. The grimacing False Faces used in the curing
rites of the False Face Society are especially
notable wooden portraits: apparitions that appear
in dreams, who, the Iroquois say, lived only
a little while ago in the far rocky regions at the rim of the earth
or wandered in the forests.

Bilingual

In the old days, she
said, we did not know those
foreign words:
stomach, lung, liver. Did not know what
sickness was. You just went to bed

and you died. I have become
third person to myself, unrecognizable
in surgical syllables, a language life
form, parallel universe that snapped
into place the first left turn I took

into the hospital. Only a sick woman
knows her tender organs
are held by an apron of fatty tissue tied
in the quaint excess of old world
vowels: oementum. Or that

the Pouch of Douglas, hidden
space between
rectum and uterus is named, sweetly,
after a parsimonious Scots surgeon who discovered it
the way Columbus claimed

America. Names for the poison
that pours in, drugs that sound like Mexican
time-shares, or maybe drinks with an umbrella
you can't believe you ordered
from the swim-up bar. It's not

the nouns, the naming
like a two-year old – *what is?* – it's that
the nouns propel me, like Alice, toward
a bumpy playing field hidden
behind an ordinary hill. In an eyeblink, it makes

some kind of sense to catch
a red flamingo by the knees, swing
wildly at new little word balls
clicking together in the underbrush or jammed
under sorry sagging hoops pestered

in the turf. Learn rules as you break
them, and it is amazing, says
the woman beside me in the white
waiting room, just what the hell
you find yourself getting used to.

March 2002

1.

A hard gurney in emergency
wilted blue curtains, smoke wall privacy,
I watch an old Cree kookum's moccasins
move to the bedside of a young man drunkpoisoned:
nephew, grandchild, someone's broken son moaning
and me unable to turn myself
from the bedside roses, legging strapped
against this foul late winter night.

This much I saw and heard: Cree wounds breaking
open beside my own.

And I am mortified by my unruly eyes and ears.

2.

Brown heels squeak on the tile, cheap shower curtain
scrapes and I turn my head, lean up on
one elbow. His nametag:
Department of Gynecological Oncology
Tom Baker Cancer Centre.
We do not shake hands and all ache
save my own falls away,
enough to hear, and all the world within eyeshot
of those fine brown shoes: *advanced ovarian cancer*

3.

Did Afghani women and children I overhear
on the dinner news feel like this
as they piled up along the Pakistani border?
Or Iraqi mothers keening by the road, blood
babies at their breasts,
or ones in Prague and Dresden summer flood ravaged,
who found out everything
was wrecked and not believing yet that it was their lives
roaring downstream, smashing
against bridge abutments and leaking through sandbags?

Prairie girls get sunburns

1.

First erotic treat: long thighs
and back bone tingling hot against the cool
white sheets tight
across my single bed.

2.

We knew better, scorned the foreign smear
of sunscreen, ugly sensible hats, squinted
straight into the glare of August, lost
by the dozen the down-to-earth dark
glasses calibrated to some damned UV index or another
by a fish-bellied scientist.

Knew evenings with friends, dangling
our sandaled feet, pushing companionably against the edges
of each other's mottled peeling skin

3.

Your arm draws underneath your breasts
needles, tubes and tape that tear your red flaking
flesh. The oxygen mask bites
sweaty ridges into your ruddy cheeks, and everyone
remarks how good your colour is. You got that burn
watching your son play ball, hit hard round third,

slide home. In this cold place,
the hot sharp air of summer
remembers you.

We did not come to remain whole
We came to lose our leaves like the trees
The trees that are broken
And start again, drawing up from the great
   roots

— ROBERT BLY

The Mind of Death

An old nightie pulling over
my bald head
tows me
back, back –

Friday nights, The Shadow's chuckle
claws its bony fingers through the grate
of the Philco upright and some adult or other advances,
arms first, the body of my flannel pajama top

rucked out in front. The too-small opening
flattens my ears forward, stings, pulls
on my hair, and I struggle
to get one arm, then another into the right

sleeves, fabric knifing at my face and armpits, and someone pulls
hard on one wrist, jamming their
impatience into my shoulder socket while in the creases
of the cotton dark hot danger breathes, laughs against my neck

and down my back.
Twenty thousand times since, I've birthed
myself headlong, rehearsals, rictus to rictus
with the dark.

Licked Into Shape: Winter Kill

Before my head knows I am
full of cancer, I go on
health jags, gag on greens,
buy another gym year, really think
I'll show up. Wheeze fitness mantras:
30 pounds by Christmas, firm butt, size 10:
meet you on the track by 6.
                              Push
hard on bikes and treadmills, crunch,
crunch my swollen belly. Just one more
lap, set, circuit
and surely, surely I will feel
better, my body will
comply. I refuse

the truth: burning
bowels, bad sleep and February
drives home weeping, beaten,
searching – *where the hell is the goddamn key* –
                                       in the dark.

Naming

*Adapted from a field manual
for the identification of Alberta butterflies*

To identify the butterfly without her
beating her wings
to pieces in a jar
they place her in an insulated
lunch pack on a small patch of blue
ice for a while.

She thinks it is a cold night and slows down.

Holding Emptiness

1. Calgary, winter 2002: as days constrict and darken

Last night's hockey scores blasting
me awake
beeping microwave,
the grind
of zippers on my snowboots,
sirens, house alarmed *Away*, exit now
scraping ice from the early morning windshield –
shit it's already seven –
car barking, engine struggling to turn over,
cellphone yelling from somewhere near
the bottom of my purse,
Palm Pilot nagging like my mother:
see somebody
about that cramping gut.

2. Thanksgiving, 2004: The Museum of the American Indian
   Exhibition of Native Baskets, New York City

The long light of autumn leaves
drifting earthbound, one leathered oak brushing
gently past my shoe,
ears filling up with the scuff
of my own feet on stairs and the wooden whispered slide
of the old door against the cool marble floor inside.

My heart is taken
by surprise, sighs back
to the silent room filled
    with baskets, women woven: someone else's ancestors sculpting
    ancient space to hold against my breasts.

On Liz, Dying

Rabbits near
the building where I work, late
October mornings or in short homeward
light, haunch hesitant
at the corner of the path
I walk every day
and do not know
rabbit-wise.

Their dun earth-brown summer
hair erases with the discipline
of white upcoming.

And so it is with you. Body skins of earth and fire and water
retreat to death-wax white

And your shivering breath
Melts you
        Into the nearby darkness
        An eyeblink universe away

Butterfly Effect

Astonishment is essential to a change of aspect.
And astonishment is thinking.
                       — LUDWIG WITTGENSTEIN

1.

When you sit it lands
        shuddering suncaught forewings black apex patch and white bar
on the leading edge

all trembles
into stillness while you hold

your breath, melt your self
for an instant in the feathered purple Cosmos.

    Look, see, just over there –

And the four submarginal eyespots catch the movement of your
    lips

                      – It's gone.

2.

When you lay dying we
        sat as you shuddered, air-hungry rasps and the rattle of mucous
settling in your throat.

A nurse lets a tiny needle land
under the skin on your chest. It hovers

in place with a butterfly clip, your fragile
plastic anchor. We hold our breath.

   Look, see, it's over –

Our ears catch that
last whisper   tender sigh   a gentle flutter of the yellow wings

      – *She's gone.*

To sit among the rocks before I die
and hear the ocean breathe

One ordinary afternoon, you
show up in my foothills office, tell me
about your new place on a magic
         spit jutting hard into the Atlantic
and of the spring migration
               of whales
      two, four, maybe
            five hundred at a time.

Use your own body
to teach my landlocked ears
the whooosssshhh and ufffhunh
           of blowholes,
                  wave and air eruptions
rolling on and on and on
        crashing against the clatter
of my humdrum life.

I look for little miracles these days

A robin nesting deep in hidden eaves,
or hyacinths, erupting through the leaves
that rot and wisp to lace. The kid who plays
alone beside my house, his everyday
unhappiness suspended as he weaves
fall flower roofs and blankets he believes
protect the lives of fairies who will stay
as long as he can be a watchful guard.

It's like a dance, the spiny sway of death
and pain and ordinary griefs held fast
in the tight embrace of love that eases scarred
and aching wounds. With every breath
I lean into this lesson: movement lasts.

False Face: Rise

Two local poets I've never heard of, Chick and Cindy, post a call for poems from cancer survivors. Upbeat, inspirational pieces. No references to God. No swearing. Am I interested? Some days all Job, I am held together by prayers and curses, weeping grief sores. Upbeat? Inspired? Fucksake – Jesus, God – how can that come to be? My words seek out iambic rhythms of the heart *lub dub, lub dub*. Line cadences *inspiration, expiration* beat witness to the inevitable caesura as the last body breath sighs and those gathered near suspend their own in hope that once more, at least, the chest will rise.

*Perhaps the self-same song that found a path
Through the sad heart of Ruth, when, sick
  for home,
She stood in tears amid the alien corn*

— JOHN KEATS

Sitting With Catherine

The old monks sat
cross-legged in charnel grounds, the edges
of their saffron robes brushing
against strong arm bones, skulls

and tufts of hair, breathing
in death, the look of it, the stench, the mundane
nightmare that keeps me restless
long into the night. And now

I sit with you, just so, leaning forward
in my chair to catch your whisper,
your steady eyes already set
west, and I am

strangely comforted by our easy talk
of dying. Your work is almost done, you say,
only one unfinished piece remains: to labour
out of failing flesh.

I gather up my things to go,
hold you close, receive
in my own bones and skin and aching
throat, the teaching:

You can't stay long.

Hagiography

Your hands rest on red
flannel pajamas while outside
your window the strong
afternoon light of early spring
folds across your bed.

I remember pictures of medieval saints.

Cords and veins strain against skin that seems
too frail to hold them. Long
fingers stroke the cloth.
Nails gently shaped: You or someone
who loves you still

attends to these small body needs.

But your wrists: bone and tendon sculptures
marbled blue with tender lines of heart
blood, strong and clear
as plainsong.
I hear your shallow breath, know

your spotless shirt hides the oozing

wound through which lung fluid
squeezes. And I feel quietly
for my own pulse, iambic transubstantiation
of breath to blood. Connected
to you in that little moment,

my own breath stops.

The mystics say that chants, stripped
to pure melody, are a sung Bible, revealing
gifts of God
in full coherence. I know that
your hands are just like that – gaunt, perfect

testaments to everything time bound.

Against Time

Laughed my way in one Thursday wearing
a black silk blouse with huge flamingoes, blue
ocean, waving palm trees: everything. Twirled
on tiptoes, and if it hadn't cost a week's wages I'd have let
you get away with calling it
my bowling shirt.

We roared like girls huddled in the back
booth of the café, sipping root beer
floats, shrieking
at our own sweet brilliance.

Shopping therapy, we said. I rolled my eyes,
slapped my right hand to my heart, swore
an oath: "Life is too damned short
for ugly clothes."

Then you spoke of death, money, each penny
you counted against the time you would
be gone. Underneath, an oily, darker current
of betrayal. Steroid swollen and sickening, how
could we love ourselves enough again to trust small
body pleasures: a lover's touch, satin
soft against a thigh?

But look, you said, hiking the hem
of your shapeless denim skirt:
strappy sandals,
extravagant, defiant.
Red.

Covered head

You wore the damned thing all the time,
even in hospital, trapped
for a week. Hair should have been the last

of your worries and still you wore that wig,
taking it off only before you slept, and quietly
warning your roommate so if she woke

in the night to pee she wouldn't be afraid
when she saw your bald head on the pillow.
Cancer good-girl whistling bravely

into the dark even as the blood clot forming
in your thigh shoved you close to death. Why
didn't you take a stand, get political, go topless,

wear a hat only to keep the weather off?

> And then I remember hobbling down the same hall
> hours after surgery, savagely determined. On one of the aching
> circuits I met an old woman sitting in the sun. We chatted, I liked
> her, tried hard not to stare at the gap where one front tooth
> had fallen out.
>
> I had the same surgeon as you to do my ovaries, she said.
> Do you know I had breast surgery at exactly the same time?
> Same table. Last year. Two docs for the price of one,
> I guess. Did you ever hear of such a thing?
> He told me I was his success story, your guy. But,
>
> it's back. It came back, and I don't know what I'll do.

27

*And I remember I stopped talking, steered
my pole and tubes and monitors
the other way
whenever I caught sight of her purple dressing gown.*

Shamed by this cruelty, humbled
by the compassion of your covered head, I now understand
warriors come differently disguised.

Kin

1.

Tiny Chinese grandmother, nested
on a chemo bed,
knees pulled up hard against the pilled green wool
of her shapeless sweater, wisps
of peppered hair pulled back against her pale skull.

I want to reach across and stroke her head,
cancer daughter in this foreign place.

2.

Back to the wall, she sits in a line
of welded waiting room chairs,
her feet just sweep the ground, the ropy veins of her twisted
hands
grip hard. Everything is carefully arranged: painted finger nails,
black hose, scoop-necked dress that sags
just slightly across the chest bone,

and I cannot keep myself
from staring at the mottled skin where someday soon
a morphine butterfly will surely land.

3.

She is lovely, young
a small black kerchief knotted high on the big bone
of her skull, just where your head, too,
is tethered to your spine. Anywhere but here

someone would want to talk to such a one, uncover
the travels that dropped her, kohl-eyed, exotic
into our pedestrian morning.

False Face: Clinic

Attitude: like an urban legend, taken-for-granted, that thing everybody knows, everybody believes, but nobody can say where they heard it in the first place. And it doesn't go away. A woman in Clinic: *Sixty percent of recovery, you know, depends on attitude. Keep positive. Just look at me. If the docs told me I had a recurrence, I'd look them straight in the eye and say: No way. You got the wrong gal.* Plies me with home remedies: electric tumor zapping, cottage cheese. Flax seed.

Two years later, I see her name in a death notice.

Not only are the depths of the female pelvis a considerable distance from the abdominal wound through which the gynaecological surgeon operates but it is also one of the more congested parts of the human body.

— PAT SOUTTER

Bald

1. Sitting Around Gossiping

A woman, propped up on her elbows
on the examination table, paper rucked up against her backside
asks the shining softness of his head: How the hell
do you stand this?

Stand what?

That we never get older, only sicker.
He peered over the top of his glasses, touched
the long bone of her leg, smiled. Well, here's the thing:
I really like bald women.

I love the flirty, fizzy chance floating
somewhere out in space that men might
still find ways to hold us in their gaze,
just as we are.

2. Months later, my own hair back, finally needing a decent cut.

The newcomer took off her wooly cap. It came out
really fast, she said, even before the second treatment. So
my son shaved off the rest. Hurt etched
her eye bones into dark craters and she looked across

the room, caught the gleam of light
from someone else's curls. Oh god, can I please
touch your hair. Just let me touch it.
Buried her face in the excess, breathing in,

breathing out, just once. And the stranger
reached up with both hands and cradled
the back of the naked head. Hey, girl, you got that Velcro
thing happening. You know, I kind of miss it.

They touched foreheads like Maori warriors.

I really like bald women.

Ragged purple scar

remember this for me: thin belly
slice, eight inches from navel to pubic bone.
Skin and fat separate in slow motion,
a stranger's hands in latex,
inside.

Who is this man who opens women up?
A drinker? Someone who fought
with his wife, slammed
out of the house that morning? What's
a shitty day at his office – did he drop

his briefcase heavily by the front door in the clutter
of teenage skates and blades?
Is he bored? Desperate for a long vacation
that should have started yesterday?

And this ragged purple scar, trailing
south southeast: a nervous
intern's slash or a precise
correction line, life-saving midline detour?

Who can say, dead
to the world?

Drowning

They don't mean it, after,
the ones who cut you open,
distant near the bed,
talking about what they did, what
they saw. Don't mean poetry
but blessedly, they find it.

Your tumors wept
into your belly, they tell me.
It's ascites. And for an instant I imagine
a tough goddess, water-born.

Remembering themselves, their talk slips
back to draining, debulking, aggressive
chemotherapy, drips, catheters. Many syllables, the flat
sharp shorthand of charts, orders.

Weeping
inside, I am
drowning.

Look Good, Feel Better

Fight with scalpels, poison drugs
that melt your eyebrows, fight
for your life with red lipstick, a new mascara wand
and Hallmark.

Keep up appearances,
make your self
                up.

Squeeze into the iron maiden of positive thinking
the way you used to squeeze into girdles, pointy-cup bras,
into not being
depressed, lonely, scared, bald, aching
in the knees and hips.

Positive has you on a leash like a long-eared
spaniel, panting, eager to please, rubbing against the legs
of strangers, hoping for a scratch behind the ears, a good
test result, a promise:
really, it's going to be all right.

Push aside everything hard and scaly
and run for your life,
bad girl, bitchy scared crabby numb
bad girl.
Dead girl.

Hands

Don't let them touch you down there
my mother warned, her tiny hands
fluttering vaguely south, casting

useless spells to keep the boys off. So of course
I did, sometimes in scruffy walk-ups, sometimes
dangerously, wildly in hot gullies, pressed

hard against the scabbed sharp skin of poplars
blackened by foraging herds
of deer, white bums poised for takeoff

through the underbrush. Today he pulls
the goose neck closer
for a better look, prods carefully, one gloved hand pressed

hard against my belly, feeling me
for crusts of tumor seeds
and rigid fluid timbre.

Still nice and soft, he smiles, rolling the latex
back, and tears he takes for gratitude
slide from my eyes.

Terra intima

They say your uterus looks like a pear, or maybe
a clenched fist,
But I see Judy Chicago inside,
a tiny headless woman womb with tubes outstretched
like Hallelujah arms,
a kind of matrioshka nested deep,
ancient goddess homuncula
blade sacrificed in the violated dark.

The female pelvis is a traffic jam, they say,
But my mind's own eye sees
Georgia O'Keefe bleached-bone
sockets that bulge with turquoise
desert sky like blistered eggs.

Mustard Gas

Returning home from France,
their throats and lungs burned out, spent soldiers share
my life: bone-cracked exhaustion, baldness, retching, mouth sores
    and the curse
of cramping diarrhea.

It took some smart American nerve gas scientists to put
two and two together over coffee, I imagine, brewed
    on Bunsen flames.
Guts and hair grow fast. As do cancer cells, so: why not? When
    we're finished
with the Germans we can hit that other fucking shit, no?

My television shouts Iraq but I don't need to travel half a world
away for the chemistry of mass destruction. My only hope
for survival squats in the sterile fluorescence of the Cancer Day
Care unit ten kilometres from my home, waiting.

Venous Refusals

The morning the nurses cannot find
a vein, they prod and dig four times, and I ball
my fingers into a useless, tight fist hoping
to raise a bulge

that will do. Like addicts shooting up
in alleys, nurses are not so innocent: try
forearms, pull back skin on my hands, stare
over bifocals for the backflow of blood

telling them I'll be mainlining poison. Veins
collapse, turn ropy through the body
and a small ruby wound inside the silk bend
of my right elbow signals

layers and layers of scarring, insult
to the slippery, gossamer, ragged
instability of the body's fine tubing. Lying
in a worn blue clinic gown, heels pressed

together, knees spread again, I comfort
the yellowing stain of another bruise, treasure
these venous refusals, the dark, moist
pulse beneath my skin.

Did you ever say Yes to one joy? O my friends, then you have also said Yes to all woe as well. All things are chained, entwined together, all things are in love.

— NIETZSCHE

Sitting in a coffee shop, cold

hands wrapped around a bowl of latte,
soy, against the troubles of my gut, drafts shivering low
on my neck, I lean away from the old window, single-paned, frost
etched against the glass, crusting edges of the peeling
wooden frame. The way I recall my childhood room
where I pressed my face against those three
holes near the sill, struggled to see out.

Nerve damage now sends my hands and feet
to agonies of itching, burning
numbness, the same as when I froze
my feet skating, wooden and clumsy, rocking
on blade guards all the way
home in twenty below dark, white
fingers clenched inside my frosted wool mittens
fire-thawed as teary cold withdrew.

Vowels

Bald women sink back
into white pillows,
lashless bird eyes fade
into skulls. Mostly, we sleep, surrendering
to chemistry's confusion, abandoning visitors
to their crosswords or tiny
daytime TV shows beamed quietly

from worlds away. But sometimes I struggle
for consciousness, laying down
one syllable after another like an anxious drunk
while the current of conversation curls
and I try to follow, stumbling on the drugs
to retrieve words mid-sentence. Nouns elude, but
from nowhere, I recall

I used to stick my head inside
the empty washer when I was a child,
singing big vowel sounds, delighting
in the slow bass resonance filling
my whole head. The same vowels we learn
to sing in grief, in pain.

False Face: Bedside

The old woman across from me – terminal, pancreatic – can ring and ring for attention before a nurse comes. When I press the button, someone is at my side in an instant. I am grateful, deeply frightened: when will my ring become "*oh her again*"? Through the drawn curtains, I hear a nurse changing the bed next to mine. *Those flowers she always gets over there are so stinky, they make me sick. Staff can't bear to come into her room to do her vitals, you know. Why don't people think of nurses when they send these damned things*? An hour later, she comes to check the sanitary pad into which my body weeps. She does not ask my friends to leave, those same friends who bring flowers, but yanks at my panties like a soiled diaper, shoves the wet cotton aside, says not one word.

Sometimes you miss people for the damndest reasons

Catherine called her wig Alice,
stuffed her into drawers and carry-ons,
hauled her out whenever
she needed not to scare clients or
be pulled over by Security because
her mugshot didn't match her head.

We teased Alice, swore at
our own itchy inability to keep the damned
things on our heads for more
than twenty minutes at a shot. And I wanted
to sponsor a drag queen
in the next run for the cure.

I ache to call her up today, howl
together at this new thing I learned
about merkins, little crotch wigs
the rich used to wear when Shakespeare
was a kid, to keep from scratching

at sores, lice bites, and she'd say:
Christ, can't you just see it? Some boozed-up
old Falstaff bringing down the house, stumbling
into the arms of Mistress Quickly wearing only
her merkin for a beard?

Kathy, barrel-assing down a back road

swinging the Stones tickets in her right hand
like a joint, pounding on the wheel
to keep up with Mick

when this twelve-year-old
cop pulls her over and starts
to scold. Obviously, she's – ahem – considerably

over the speed limit. She hears the prissy whistle
of air in his nostrils as he is about
to Ma'am her, so she yanks off

her toque, and now he's staring straight
into the stubble on her head like he's just seen
Boris Karloff, or maybe his grandma naked

in the middle of the afternoon. She dusts
her hands in the direction of his retreating
backside, winks lewdly at the rear view mirror.

If you got it, girl, you flaunt it.

Cold Comfort

*It's what we have to offer, to comfort one another:
the truth of where we are, and who, and where we're headed.*
— YANN MARTEL

I find myself
here in the winter morning coffee shop, sleepy
cheek cradled in a loopy scarf knit by a friend
and here, aching on a hard bed

at three, alone. Here, kicking through
leaves, or tethered to an IV pole, poison
through slippery veins, and here, burying
a smile in two dozen perfect roses.

Sitting quietly, breathing here
just because I do, I learn
a body that grows old, disappoints
to death.

Look:
where we're headed
is charted only by true latitudes of myth
that shake us in the dark, whisper
strange pictures, rustle on our skin
and float like Dali
under the pennies on our eyes.

Winter Clarity

Of sky, tree
bones sharp edged,
pillowed snow
softening angles,
holding
but not holding on.

If hard-edged clarity is what I seek,
winter is the time for it.
Nothing is hidden.
Summer hedges close themselves
in mats of green, seem
solid, dense, true. But

winter shows me more:
each twig and branch,
berries, one by one,
skulls of last year's blossoms.

What opens up in winter
reveals itself as more
space than matter.

Licked Into Shape: January Big Bear Moon

Sickness grants the boon
of hibernation: surrender
to the weight of winter, burrow down
a nest of twigs and leaves and dreams.

Spend breath enough
only to move my heart, the den
a world inside, shaped simply
to the curve of my own spine.

The dead of winter
births hairless young, formless
flesh cradled at the breast
of one who stirs only to their

transformation. Licked slowly
into shape, the stories say,
by the rasping heat
of the sleeper's loving tongue.

Acknowledgements

I wish to acknowledge writing friends who encouraged me to share my story with strangers. First, Edna Alford, who saw some merit in these poems and extended her hand, both professionally and personally. Second, Tim Lilburn and the Fall 2004 poetry group at the Banff Centre *Writing With Style* program who helped me know that, while these poems stem from my particular experience with one disease, they speak to the transformative possibilities in any life.

And with heartfelt gratitude, Lorri Neilsen Glenn. It was Lorri who first knew that poetry was the vehicle I most needed to gather in the pieces that I am. Her encouragement and friendship in the early days of writing these poems made everything else possible. And her sure and skilful hand as an editor shaped them lovingly, and as cleanly as any surgeon's.

The quotation from Toni Morrison is from *Beloved*.

The quotation about the False Face Society is from Oracle Series, no. 125, "False Face Curing Society."

The lines from Robert Bly are from "A Home in Dark Grass" from *The Light Around the Body*.

"Naming" is adapted from "Tips on Learning to Identify Alberta Butterflies," Beck, Barb and Beck, Jim (1999), used by permission of the authors.

The quotation from Ludwig Wittgenstein is from *Last Writings on the Philosophy of Psychology, Vol. 1.* G.H. von Wright and Heikki Nyman (Eds.) trans. C.G. Luckhardt and M.A.E. Aue, Chicago: Chicago University Press.

The lines from John Keats are from "Ode to a Nightingale."

The quotation from Pat Soutter is from "Gynecological Surgery and Oncology" and is used by permission of the author.

The quotation from Friederich Nietschze is from *Thus Spake Zarathustra*, trans. R.J. Hollingdale, Penguin Classics.

The quotation from Yann Martel is from *Fast Forward* and is used by permission of the publisher.

About the Author

Pat Clifford is a teacher, education consultant, and researcher. She has published widely in academic journals and books. *Embracing Brings You Back* is her first book of poetry. Raised in Saskatoon, she has been writing since her days in school – but it is her experience of living with recurrent ovarian cancer that provided the impetus to return to poetry after too many years' absence. She has lived Calgary since 1976.